Fluorescent Activity Books

NEON NATURE
COLOURING & STICKER
ACTIVITY BOOK

BY SAM **HUTCHINSON**
DESIGNED & **ILLUSTRATED** BY **VICKY** BARKER

www.bsmall.co.uk

Published by b small publishing ltd.
Text and illustrations copyright © b small publishing ltd. 2016 • 3 4 5 • ISBN 97 8-1-909767-63-8
Production by Madeleine Ehm. Printed in Malaysia by Thumbprints Utd.

ABOUT THIS BOOK

In nature, some animals and plants have chemicals in their body
that they can use to create a glow.

This is called **bioluminescence.**

The creatures on these pages look decidedly black and white...
They need your help to brighten them up. Using some bright
or fluorescent colouring pens and the stickers at the back
of the book, bring these scenes to life on the page.
Read the introduction on each page to learn a little
more about neon in nature.

DEEP-SEA CREATURES

DEEP-SEA CREATURES

Down in the deep of the ocean, where light cannot reach, the creatures that live there have developed the ability to glow in the dark. These fish live in a harsh and tough environment. So harsh, in fact, that it's quite difficult for humans to visit them in order to study more about them. This means that these creatures are very mysterious and it is hard to know exactly why they have developed this ability. One suggestion is that the fish might glow to attract their prey. Can you think of any other reasons why it might be useful?

Colour in the creatures opposite using bright colouring pens or highlighters.
Use the stickers to add fluorescent flashes.

Fold out this scene

FIREFLIES

FIREFLIES

Fireflies are a type of winged beetle and most of them can glow through bioluminescence (see page 2). The ones that cannot glow are diurnal, which means that they are active during the day (this is the opposite of nocturnal) so they don't need to glow. The nocturnal types, which are active at night, use their glow to attract mates or prey in the dark. One particularly sneaky type of firefly attracts smaller types with a friendly glow and then eats them! Baby fireflies are born as larvae and they can also glow.

They are called **glowworms**.

Using your colouring pens and the stickers at the back of the book, help the fireflies on the page opposite to glow. They usually glow yellow, green or pale red.

Fold out this scene

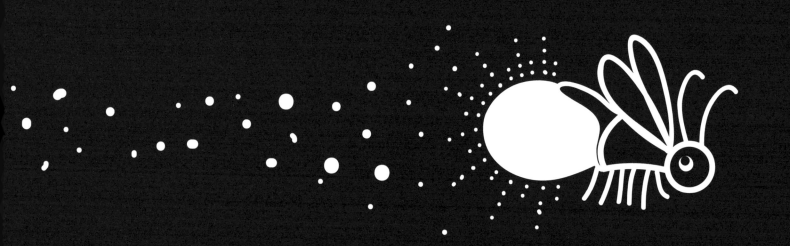

THE CEPHALOPOD

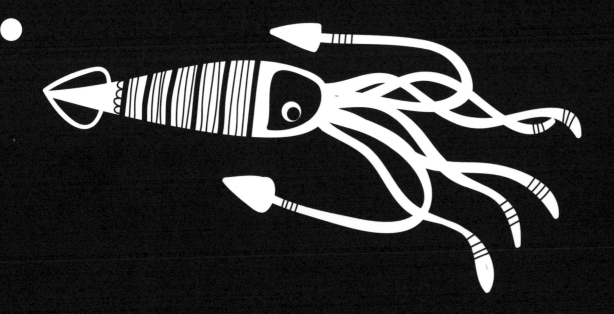

THE CEPHALOPOD

The word cephalopod comes from the Greek for 'head-feet'. Common types of cephalopod include octopuses, squid and cuttlefish. The Greek meaning behind the word makes sense because they are mostly head and feet! There are many different species of cephalopod and they can be found in oceans all around the world. Like the deep-sea creatures on page 3, scientists aren't quite certain whether cephalopods glow to attract their prey or to disguise their own shadow to stop them becoming something else's prey. It might even be possible that they glow to communicate with each other.

What are the cephalopods on the opposite page trying to say to each other? Use your colouring pens and the stickers at the back of the book to help them talk to each other. Maybe your cephalopods will glow a certain colour when they are angry and a different colour to say hello.

Fold out this scene

CORAL REEFS

CORAL REEFS

Coral reefs are full of beautiful colours and fish.
They look like complicated rock structures but they are
actually made up of animals, called corals, and plants,

called algae, that grow together symbiotically
(this means that they need each other!).

These are the only creatures in this book that are not
bioluminescent, they are fluorescent. This means that
they reflect glowing light if you shine a specific kind
of UV light on them instead of being able to create their
own light that we can see.

Pretend that you are diving in a tropical see and are
shining your UV light on the coral reef opposite.
Bring it to life with your colouring pens and the
stickers at the back of the book.

Fold out this scene

GLOW-IN-THE-DARK TREES

GLOW-IN-THE-DARK TREES

Nature, art and design could all work together one day, according to research by students at university, to create plants and trees that glow in the dark. Using the organisms that help animals like cephalopods and fireflies to glow, scientists can capture their ability and give it to trees and plants.

It is unlikely that a tree could make enough light to replace a street light but it would certainly look very futuristic to have glowing trees in a city. You could even have a glowing plant in your room at night. Some scientists are worried about the idea of playing with nature in this way because we don't know what the consequences will be.

Illuminate this city at night using your pens and the stickers at the back of the book.

Fold out this scene